Introduction

The people we call the Romans lived in the **Roman Empire** thousands of years ago. The Romans lived in Italy and many other countries, too. The Roman army was often fighting to gain more land. At one stage the Roman Empire covered all of the Mediterranean, parts of the Middle East, Britain and part of northern Africa. Thirty countries were part of the Roman Empire. Many millions of people lived in those countries.

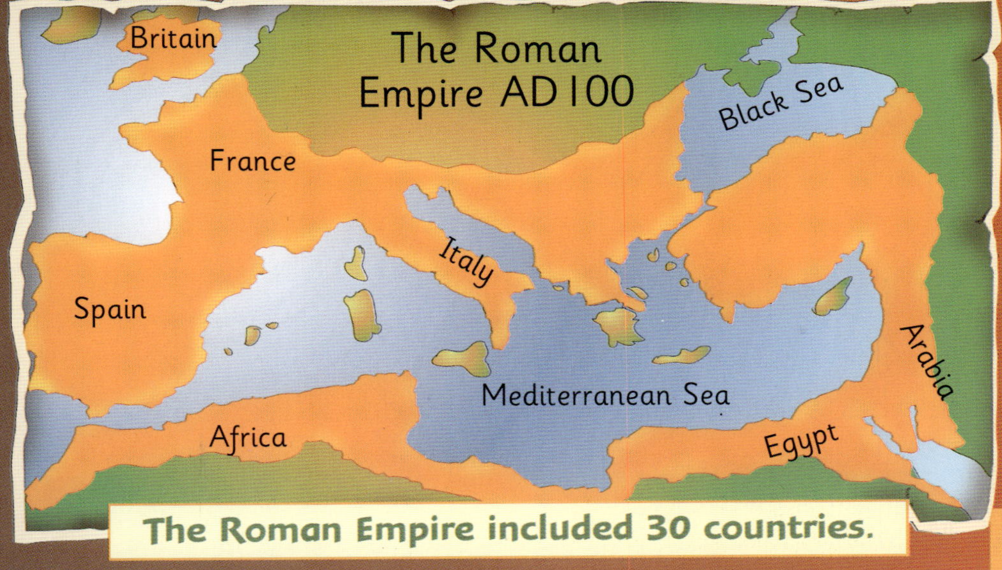

The Roman Empire included 30 countries.

Society in Ancient Rome

Romans were divided into groups, based on wealth. These groups were called patricians, equites, plebians and slaves. Each group was allowed to do different things.

OXFORD
UNIVERSITY PRESS

Romans

Anne-Marie Parker

Contents

Roman Empire Social Groups

	Schooling	Jobs	Wealth	Home
Patricians	most went to school	senators lawyers landowners	very rich	large houses second country home other land
Equites	most went to school	businessmen teachers	rich	large houses
Plebians	some went to school	traders soldiers	not very rich	small houses or no home
Slaves	none went to school	cooking cleaning farming	poor	no homes of their own lived with patricians or equites

The Romans had slaves and were usually very mean to them. Slaves were whipped and kept in chains. They were not given many clothes and were often hungry. Slaves were captured from countries that the Romans **invaded**. Slaves did most of the work in towns and cities.

A slave market

Slaves were bought and sold at slave markets. Many slaves were still children. However, some slaves were set free by their masters when they were older. Sometimes, if they earned enough money, they were able to buy their freedom.

The Roman Calendar

Our calendar is based on the Roman calendar. It has 12 months and 365 days.

The first Roman calendar only had 10 months. The first month was March and the tenth was December. 'Decem' is the Latin word for ten. Latin is the language the Romans used. The names of some of the other months also showed which number they were. But later the Romans added in the months January and February at the beginning of the year. So the numbers of the months do not match their names any more.

Number	Latin word for number	Month
7	septem	September
8	octo	October
9	novem	November
10	decem	December

Living in the City

Some city houses were very large and very grand. They were owned by wealthy patrician families. Slaves lived there, too. The slaves cooked and cleaned. They made sure that the family was well looked after.

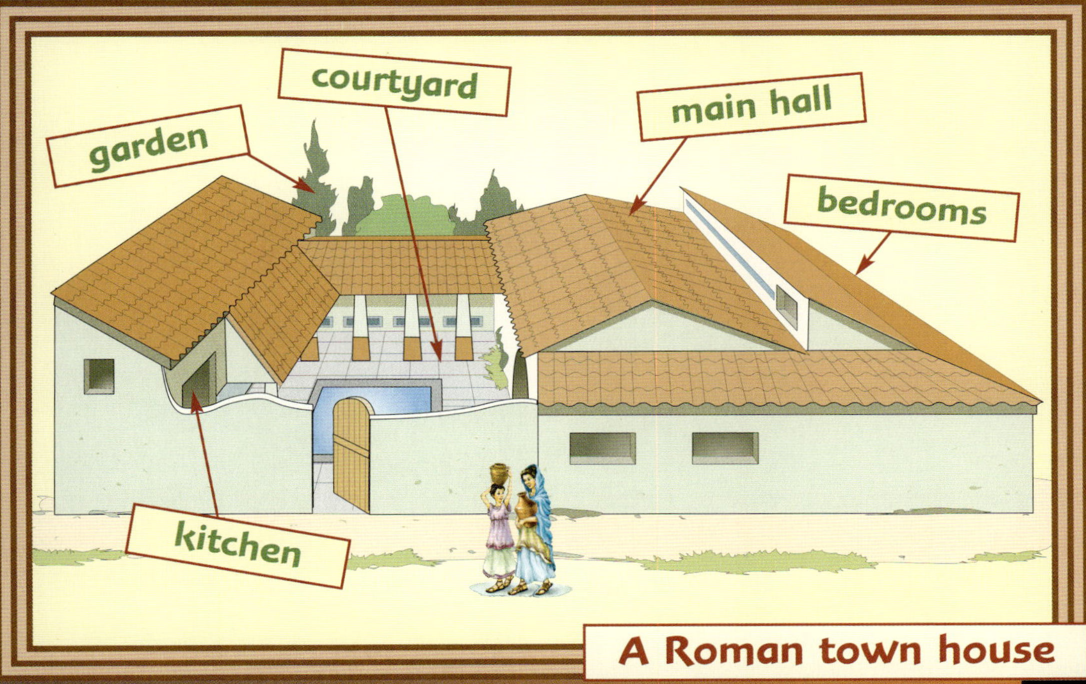

A Roman town house

Poorer families in the city lived in homes called **insulas,** which were like flats. Sometimes they were just one room. Most of them did not have a kitchen or a bathroom. But the Romans built public toilets and bath-houses in all their big towns for everybody to use.

Living in the Country

Many wealthy Roman families had a house in the country called a villa. Many villas had farms looked after by slaves. They grew onions, olives, grapes, leeks and wheat. They also bred pigs, sheep and cattle.

A family would visit their country house to get away from the heat of the city in summer.

This Roman villa had a **mosaic** floor.

Eating and Drinking

Most Romans ate their main meal in the afternoon. They ate with little spoons or with their hands. For wealthy families, this meal would have had at least three courses. For poor families, the meal may have been just one simple vegetable dish.

A Roman feast

Wealthy families had big kitchens and slaves to cook their food. Poor families did not have kitchens in their homes so they bought hot food from the street stalls.

Romans were famous for their huge feasts. They loved to show off their money and eat unusual things like snails, swans, crows, horses and peacocks.

At some feasts, Romans ate until they were sick. There would be a special room to be sick in and then they would come back to the feast and carry on eating.

Romans did not have tea or coffee. They drank wine with water in it. Only children and people who were ill drank milk.

Clothing

Roman women and girls wore long tunics underneath dresses. Wealthy women also wore make-up and jewellery, and had slaves to style their hair.

Men and boys wore short tunics. Important men wore togas over their tunics. Togas were made out of one long piece of cloth draped around the body. They could be very hot to wear. Boys were allowed to wear special togas when they were 14 years old, to show that they were now men.

Boots and sandals were made out of leather and came in many different styles.

Keeping Clean

Wealthy Roman families had baths in their homes. Other people had to use public baths. Slaves lit fires to heat the water for the baths. The public baths were for keeping clean, but they were for lots of other things, too. People went to the baths to see their friends, play games and exercise.

    People did not wash with soap. They had a different way of cleaning themselves. They went into a hot room with lots of steam. They rubbed olive oil on their bodies and then scraped it off. Finally, they went into a cold room or cold bath.

    Romans used powdered mouse brains to clean their teeth!

Going to School

No one can be sure just how many Roman children went to school, but not all Romans could read or write.

Children who did go to school began when they were about six or seven. Boys could keep going to school after the age of twelve. Teenage girls stayed at home with their mothers.

Children did not have pens or paper. They wrote on wax tablets and did sums on an **abacus**.

Here are some Roman numbers.
I=1 V=5 X=10 L=50 C=100

Here is a Roman sum.
LXXXVIII + XII=C

Ask your teacher how to work out the answer.

Roman children learned the language of the **Roman Empire**, which was Latin.

Some Latin words are very similar to the English language we use today.

Latin words carved into a stone tablet

Playing Games

Patrician Roman children had lots of time to play games or play with their pets. Slave children did not have so much time to play as they were too busy working.

Today, people still play some games that Roman children played, like marbles. Roman marbles were made out of pottery or glass.

Roman children also played other games you may know, like hide and seek, chase, hopscotch, and leapfrog. They had swings, kites, building blocks and dolls.

Roman marbles

Roman women playing a game of knucklebones

Dolls were made out of rags, wood or clay. Other games that were popular included rolling a hoop with a stick, playing ball and playing knucklebones, which is like our game of jacks.

The Chariot Races

Thousands of Romans went to watch **chariot** races. They loved the excitement of the races. They shouted and yelled when the chariots sped around corners, tilted onto just one wheel, and when they crashed.

Chariots were pulled by horses, sometimes two and sometimes four. The chariot driver was called the charioteer. It was the charioteer's job to make the horses go as fast as they could around a special track. After seven laps, they crossed the finish line. The winner of the race was given a crown of leaves and a purse of gold.

A Roman chariot race

Glossary

abacus – A tool made up of a number of bars with wooden counters on them, used for counting and maths.

chariot – A wooden carriage that was pulled by horses and driven by a charioteer, often used in races.

insula – Four or five-storey building built like a block of flats, so that many people could live in a small area.

invade – Enter a country to take control of it.

mosaic – A picture made of tiny coloured stones.

Roman Empire – All the lands that were ruled by the Romans.

Index